made by

Jürgen Pott

Professional MVP Development

things to consider

A **workbook** for the **rapid** and **professional** development of impeccable MVPs for product management and anyone involved with products.

Questions?

info@theSTRIDESPath.de

- Version: 1.0
- Date: 09.05.2019

- ISBN 13: 978-1097572496

designed in Germany

Content

PROBLEM?

- What's the problem?
- Who does the problem concern?
- Is the problem heavy enough?
- How many does the problem affect?
- Has the problem already been solved?

WHAT IS THE PROBLEM?

DESCRIBE THE PROBLEM IN SHORT TERMS.

WHO HAS THE **PROBLEM?**

WHICH PEOPLE HAVE THIS PROBLEM.

A-LEVEL customer / persona

A-LEVEL customer / persona

A-LEVEL customer / persona

B-LEVEL customer

B-LEVEL customer

C-LEVEL customer

INTERVIEW YOUR PARTNER!

INTERVIEW 3 PEOPLES, SWAP ROLES, REPEAT & TAKE NOTES

WHAT IS THE MOST **PAIN**?

WHAT IS THE GREATEST PAIN WITH THE CURRENT SOLUTION?

WHAT WORKS **WELL** SO FAR?

DESCRIBE WHAT IS GOING WELL SO FAR.

WHAT IS THE CURRENT **BENEFIT**?

DESCRIBE WHY THE CURRENT SOLUTION WORKS / EXISTS.

IDEA

- What's the idea?
- What is so special about the idea?
- Does this idea already exist?
- How can the idea be extended?

WHAT IS THE IDEA?

DESCRIBE THE IDEA YOU HAVE IN YOUR MIND.

CAPTURE MOST IMPORTANT **FINDINGS!**

WHAT DID YOU LEARNED ABOUT THE PROBLEM & THE IDEA?

Goals & Wishes

Feelings & Motivation

What do you SEE & what do you not SEE?

DEVELOP RADICAL NEW IDEAS?

WRITE MORE IDEAS, FEATURES OR DIFFERENT PARTS.

GET CONCRETE!

CHOOSE THE ESSENS OF YOUR IDEAS AND MAKE IT CONCRETE!

Hello!
NAME your IDEA

We have a problem.
Which **problem / customer needs** is **focused** by your idea?

Innovation.
Describe the **idea** in your own **words**.

How does it work?
Describe briefly some **details, features, functions** of your **idea**.

Sketch the idea. [short... very shortly]

SKETCH THE IDEA IN DETAIL!

SKETCH YOUR IDEA a little bit more in DETAIL.

Sketch the idea.

SKETCH A DIFFERENT PERSPECTIVE!

SKETCH YOUR IDEA FROM A DIFFERENT PERSON OR MARKET.

Sketch the idea from a different point of view.

Sketch the idea from a different point of view.

SOLUTION

- What's the solution?
- What are the benefits of the solution?
- What does the solution consist of?
- Are there any limitations?
- What is special about the solution?

BUILD A SOLUTION!

CREATE A PROTOTYPE YOUR PARTNER CAN INTERACT WITH.

DEVELOP OR CONSTRUATE a simple Prototype or MVP. [but not HERE] ... in real.

COLLECT **FEEDBACK?**

SHARE YOUR SOLUTION AND GET FEEDBACK.

WHAT **WORKS?**

WHAT CAN BE **IMPROVED?**

OPEN **QUESTIONS?**

ANY **IDEAS?**

WHAT DID YOU NEED?

TO CREATE THE PROTOTYPE.

TECHNOLOGY: What type of technology do you need to develop / construate the solution?

SERVICES: What services do you need to construate / provide the solution?

QUALIFICATION: What qualifications do you need to construate / provide the solution?

MATERIAL: What material do you need to construate / provide the solution?

TIME & MONEY: What does the prototype cost? And how long did it take to develop the prototype?

WHAT DID YOU LEARN!

NOTE DOWN, WHAT COMES TO YOUR MIND.

NOTE DOWN, what you spontaniously learned about the creation of your prototype.

VALUE

- What are the benefits of the product?
- What benefit is needed on the market?
- What are the benefits of other products?
- How do I create the right benefit?

WHAT IS THE **BENEFIT** OF THE **SOLUTION?**

NOTE THE *most important / overall* BENEFIT.

NOTE SPECIFIC BENEFITS!

NOTE specific BENEFITs for specific CUSTOMERs.

A-Level customer / persona

B-Level customer

C-Level customer

WHAT ARE THE **USE CASES**?

DESCRIBE WHICH USE CASES ARE POSSIBLE WITH THE PRODUCT

A-Level customer / persona / PRIMARY

A-Level customer / persona / SECONDARY

WHAT ARE THE **USE CASES**?

DESCRIBE WHICH USE CASES ARE POSSIBLE WITH THE PRODUCT

B-Level customer

C-Level customer

CUSTOMER / PERSONA

- Who uses my product?
- What benefits do these people need?
- How can the product provide benefits?
- What problems do these people have?
- What tasks do these people have to perform?

WHO ARE THE CUSTOMERs?

WHICH PERSONA WANTS TO BUY THE PRODUCT?

A-LEVEL customer / persona!	**TYPE**	**SIZE**
A-LEVEL customer / persona!	**TYPE**	**SIZE**
A-LEVEL customer / persona!	**TYPE**	**SIZE**
B-LEVEL customer!		**SIZE**
B-LEVEL customer		**SIZE**
C-LEVEL customer!		

THE TYPE OF CUSTOMERs?

WHAT KIND OF CUSTOMER HAS THE PROBLEM?

TYPE: What kind of customer has the problem?

PERSONA CANVAS

A-LEVEL PERSONA

Priority PRIMARY

NAME:

AGE:

OCCUPATION:

LOCATION:

INCOME:

“ Statement

”

Job to be done: The persona job, that needs to be done?

PERSONA **FACTS**

LEARN TO UNDERSTAND THE PERSONA

PERSONALITY

EXTROVERT — INTROVERT

SENSING — INTUITION

THINKING — FEELING

JUDGING — PERCEIVING

PASSIVE — ACTIVE

GET INVOLVED

INCENTIVE

SOCIAL

ACHIEVEMENT

GROWTH

POWER

GOALS

WHERE TO REACH?

TRADITIONAL / DIRECT MAIL

ONLINE ADS / E-MAIL

BLOGS & SOCIAL MEDIA

REFERRALS

PHYSICAL LOCATIONS

PAIN POINTS

RELATIONSHIP with the PRODUCT

PERSONA TECHNOLOGY

With what does the person work and what does the person do?

TECHNOLOGY

...

DEVICES & PLATFORMS

...

FAVE brands / apps / invluencer

...

The **REASON** to use our **PRODUCT?**

The **Dealbreaker!**

BIO of the PERSONA

WRITE DOWN the INDIVIDUAL BIO of the PERSONA

BIO: The individual and significant bio topics?

“

”

FEARS: Personal issues

HOPES: Personal hopes

NEEDS: Whats does this person really want?

JOURNEY of the PERSONA

WRITE DOWN the CUSTOMER JOURNEY of the PERSONA

AWARENESS

STEPS

TOUCHPOINTS

CONSIDERATION

STEPS

TOUCHPOINTS

ACQUISITION

STEPS

TOUCHPOINTS

SERVICE

STEPS

TOUCHPOINTS

LOYALTY

STEPS

TOUCHPOINTS

PERSONA CANVAS

A-LEVEL PERSONA

Priority PRIMARY

NAME:

AGE:

OCCUPATION:

LOCATION:

INCOME:

“ Statement ”

Job to be done: The persona job, that needs to be done?

PERSONA **FACTS**

LEARN TO UNDERSTAND THE PERSONA

PERSONALITY

EXTROVERT — INTROVERT

SENSING — INTUITION

THINKING — FEELING

JUDGING — PERCEIVING

PASSIVE — ACTIVE

GET INVOLVED

INCENTIVE

SOCIAL

ACHIEVEMENT

GROWTH

POWER

GOALS

WHERE TO REACH?

TRADITIONAL / DIRECT MAIL

ONLINE ADS / E-MAIL

BLOGS & SOCIAL MEDIA

REFERRALS

PHYSICAL LOCATIONS

PAIN POINTS

RELATIONSHIP with the PRODUCT

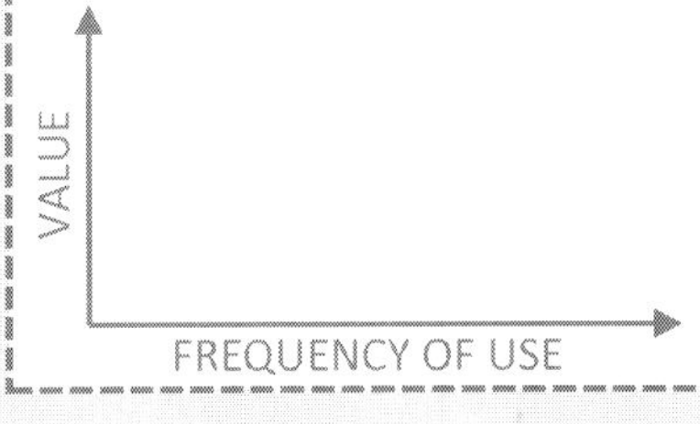

PERSONA TECHNOLOGY

With what does the person work and what does the person do?

TECHNOLOGY

...

DEVICES & PLATFORMS

...

FAVE brands / apps / invluencer

...

The REASON to use our PRODUCT?

The Dealbreaker!

BIO of the PERSONA

WRITE DOWN the INDIVIDUAL BIO of the PERSONA

BIO: The individual and significant bio topics?

“

”

NOTES: any other topics?

JOURNEY of the PERSONA

WRITE DOWN the CUSTOMER JOURNEY of the PERSONA

AWARENESS

STEPS

TOUCHPOINTS

CONSIDERATION

STEPS

TOUCHPOINTS

ACQUISITION

STEPS

TOUCHPOINTS

SERVICE	LOYALTY
STEPS	STEPS
TOUCHPOINTS	TOUCHPOINTS

PERSONA CANVAS

A-LEVEL PERSONA

Priority SECONDARY

NAME:

AGE:

OCCUPATION:

LOCATION:

INCOME:

“ Statement

”

Job to be done: The persona job, that needs to be done?

PERSONA FACTS

LEARN TO UNDERSTAND THE PERSONA

PERSONALITY

EXTROVERT — INTROVERT

SENSING — INTUITION

THINKING — FEELING

JUDGING — PERCEIVING

PASSIVE — ACTIVE

GET INVOLVED

INCENTIVE

SOCIAL

ACHIEVEMENT

GROWTH

POWER

GOALS

WHERE TO REACH?

TRADITIONAL / DIRECT MAIL

ONLINE ADS / E-MAIL

BLOGS & SOCIAL MEDIA

REFERRALS

PHYSICAL LOCATIONS

PAIN POINTS

RELATIONSHIP with the PRODUCT

PERSONA TECHNOLOGY

With what does the person work and what does the person do?

TECHNOLOGY

...

DEVICES & PLATFORMS

...

FAVE brands / apps / invluencer

...

The REASON to use our PRODUCT?

The Dealbreaker!

BIO of the PERSONA

WRITE DOWN the INDIVIDUAL BIO of the PERSONA

BIO: The individual and significant bio topics?

“

”

NOTES: any other topics?

JOURNEY of the PERSONA

WRITE DOWN the CUSTOMER JOURNEY of the PERSONA

AWARENESS

STEPS

TOUCHPOINTS

CONSIDERATION

STEPS

TOUCHPOINTS

ACQUISITION

STEPS

TOUCHPOINTS

SERVICE	LOYALTY
STEPS	STEPS
TOUCHPOINTS	TOUCHPOINTS

PERSONA CANVAS

A-LEVEL PERSONA

Priority PRIMARY

NAME:

AGE:

OCCUPATION:

LOCATION:

INCOME:

“ Statement ”

Job to be done: The persona job, that needs to be done?

PERSONA FACTS

LEARN TO UNDERSTAND THE PERSONA

PERSONALITY

EXTROVERT — INTROVERT

SENSING — INTUITION

THINKING — FEELING

JUDGING — PERCEIVING

PASSIVE — ACTIVE

GET INVOLVED

INCENTIVE

SOCIAL

ACHIEVEMENT

GROWTH

POWER

GOALS

WHERE TO REACH?

TRADITIONAL / DIRECT MAIL

ONLINE ADS / E-MAIL

BLOGS & SOCIAL MEDIA

REFERRALS

PHYSICAL LOCATIONS

PAIN POINTS

RELATIONSHIP with the PRODUCT

PERSONA TECHNOLOGY

With what does the person work and what does the person do?

TECHNOLOGY

...

DEVICES & PLATFORMS

...

FAVE brands / apps / invluencer

...

The **REASON** to use our **PRODUCT?**

The **Dealbreaker!**

BIO of the PERSONA

WRITE DOWN the INDIVIDUAL BIO of the PERSONA

BIO: The individual and significant bio topics?

“

”

NOTES: any other topics?

PERSONA CANVAS

A-LEVEL PERSONA

Priority SECONDARY

NAME:

AGE:

OCCUPATION:

LOCATION:

INCOME:

“ Statement ”

Job to be done: The persona job, that needs to be done?

PERSONA FACTS

LEARN TO UNDERSTAND THE PERSONA

PERSONALITY

EXTROVERT — INTROVERT

SENSING — INTUITION

THINKING — FEELING

JUDGING — PERCEIVING

PASSIVE — ACTIVE

GET INVOLVED

INCENTIVE

SOCIAL

ACHIEVEMENT

GROWTH

POWER

GOALS

WHERE TO REACH?

TRADITIONAL / DIRECT MAIL

ONLINE ADS / E-MAIL

BLOGS & SOCIAL MEDIA

REFERRALS

PHYSICAL LOCATIONS

PAIN POINTS

RELATIONSHIP with the PRODUCT

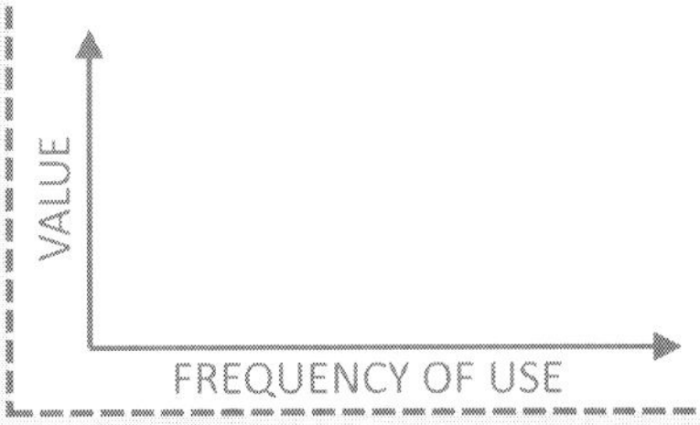

PERSONA **TECHNOLOGY**

With what does the person work and what does the person do?

TECHNOLOGY

...

DEVICES & PLATFORMS

...

FAVE brands / apps / invluencer

...

The **REASON** to use our **PRODUCT?**

The **Dealbreaker!**

BIO of the PERSONA

WRITE DOWN the INDIVIDUAL BIO of the PERSONA

BIO: The individual and significant bio topics?

“

”

NOTES: any other topics?

COMPETITORS / ALTERNATIVES

- Which competitors are there?
- Are there any competitors at all?
- What product alternatives are there?
- How good are these product alternatives?
- Is the development of a product worthwhile?

WHO ARE THE COMPETITORSs?

WHICH COMPANIES HAVE ALTERNATIVE PRODUCTS?

A-LEVEL competitor / primary

POWER

SIZE

A-LEVEL competitor / primary

POWER

SIZE

A-LEVEL competitor / secondary

POWER

SIZE

B-LEVEL competitor / primary

POWER

B-LEVEL competitor / secondary

POWER

C-LEVEL competitors

THE TYPE OF COMPETITORS?

WHAT KIND OF COMPETITORS HAVE THE ALTERNATIVES?

TYPE: What kind of COMPETITORS have the ALTERNATIVES?

COMPETITOR CANVAS

A-LEVEL COMPETITOR

Priority PRIMARY

NAME:

FOUNDATION:

EMPLOYEES:

PRODUCTS:

MONEY:

" VISION

"

Mission: The mission, that needs to be done?

CEO AND DRIVER

WHO IS THE DRIVER IN THIS COMPANY

Priority PRIMARY

NAME:

AGE:

OCCUPATION:

LOCATION:

INCOME:

“ Statement ”

Job to be done: The persona job, that needs to be done?

HIS MISSION: Why he is the DRIVER in this company?

COMPETITOR STRATEGY

HOW DOES THE COMPETITOR RECH ITS CUSTOMERS?

STRATEGY: What is the competitor´s market strategy?

MARKETING: Which marketing strategy does the competitor pursue?

PARTNER: Which partners does the competitor work with?

COMPETITOR MARKET AND SIZE

WHAT IS THE DISADVANTAGE OF THIS COMPETITOR?

MARKETS: Which markets does the competitor own or try to occupy? In which markets is he active?

SIZE & SCALING: How much market power does the competitor have and how does he scale his business?

Growth: How has the competitor´s growth changed in the past and how is it likely to change in the future?

COMPETITOR **GAINS**

WHAT IS THE ADVANTAGE OF THIS COMPETITOR?

Products: What are the product advantadges of this competitor?

Services: What are the service advantadges of this competitor?

Solutions: What are the „complete solution“ advantadges of this competitor?

COMPETITOR **PAINS**

WHAT IS THE DISADVANTAGE OF THIS COMPETITOR?

Products: What are the product advantadges of this competitor?

Services: What are the service advantadges of this competitor?

Solutions: What are the „complete solution“ advantadges of this competitor?

MOST ATTRACTIVE ALTERNATIVES

NOTE THE BEST PRODUCT ALTERNATIVES TO YOUR PRODUCT

A-Level: What is the BEST Product ALTERNATIVE of this competitor to your PRODUCT?

B-Level: What is an ACCEPTABLE Product ALTERNATIVE of this competitor to your PRODUCT?

C-Level: What is a TOLERABLE Product ALTERNATIVE of this competitor to your PRODUCT?

ALTERNATIVE **OPTIONS**

NOTE ADVANTAGES AND DISADVANTAGES of the ALTERNATIVES

A-Level: What are the advantages and disadvantages of the alternative products?

B-Level: What are the advantages and disadvantages of the alternative products?

C-Level: What are the advantages and disadvantages of the alternative products?

COMPETITOR CANVAS

A-LEVEL COMPETITOR

Priority PRIMARY

NAME:

FOUNDATION:

EMPLOYEES:

PRODUCTS:

MONEY:

“ VISION ”

Mission: The mission, that needs to be done?

CEO AND DRIVER

WHO IS THE DRIVER IN THIS COMPANY

Priority PRIMARY

NAME:

AGE:

OCCUPATION:

LOCATION:

INCOME:

“ Statement ”

Job to be done: The persona job, that needs to be done?

HIS MISSION: Why he is the DRIVER in this company?

COMPETITOR STRATEGY

HOW DOES THE COMPETITOR RECH ITS CUSTOMERS?

STRATEGY: What is the competitor´s market strategy?

MARKETING: Which marketing strategy does the competitor pursue?

PARTNER: Which partners does the competitor work with?

COMPETITOR **MARKET AND SIZE**

WHAT IS THE DISADVANTAGE OF THIS COMPETITOR?

MARKETS: Which markets does the competitor own or try to occupy? In which markets is he active?

SIZE & SCALING: How much market power does the competitor have and how does he scale his business?

Growth: How has the competitor´s growth changed in the past and how is it likely to change in the future?

COMPETITOR **GAINS**

WHAT IS THE ADVANTAGE OF THIS COMPETITOR?

Products: What are the product advantadges of this competitor?

Services: What are the service advantadges of this competitor?

Solutions: What are the „complete solution" advantadges of this competitor?

COMPETITOR **PAINS**

WHAT IS THE DISADVANTAGE OF THIS COMPETITOR?

Products: What are the product advantadges of this competitor?

Services: What are the service advantadges of this competitor?

Solutions: What are the „complete solution" advantadges of this competitor?

MOST ATTRACTIVE **ALTERNATIVES**

NOTE THE BEST PRODUCT ALTERNATIVES TO YOUR PRODUCT

A-Level: What is the BEST Product ALTERNATIVE of this competitor to your PRODUCT?

B-Level: What is an ACCEPTABLE Product ALTERNATIVE of this competitor to your PRODUCT?

C-Level: What is a TOLERABLE Product ALTERNATIVE of this competitor to your PRODUCT?

ALTERNATIVE OPTIONS

NOTE ADVANTAGES AND DISADVANTAGES of the ALTERNATIVES

A-Level: What are the advantages and disadvantages of the alternative products?

B-Level: What are the advantages and disadvantages of the alternative products?

C-Level: What are the advantages and disadvantages of the alternative products?

COMPETITOR CANVAS

A-LEVEL COMPETITOR

Priority SECONDARY

NAME:

FOUNDATION:

EMPLOYEES:

PRODUCTS:

MONEY:

“ VISION ”

Mission: The mission, that needs to be done?

CEO AND DRIVER

WHO IS THE DRIVER IN THIS COMPANY

Priority PRIMARY

NAME:

AGE:

OCCUPATION:

LOCATION:

INCOME:

“ Statement ”

Job to be done: The persona job, that needs to be done?

HIS MISSION: Why he is the DRIVER in this company?

COMPETITOR **STRATEGY**

HOW DOES THE COMPETITOR RECH ITS CUSTOMERS?

STRATEGY: What is the competitor´s market strategy?

MARKETING: Which marketing strategy does the competitor pursue?

PARTNER: Which partners does the competitor work with?

COMPETITOR **MARKET AND SIZE**

WHAT IS THE DISADVANTAGE OF THIS COMPETITOR?

MARKETS: Which markets does the competitor own or try to occupy? In which markets is he active?

SIZE & SCALING: How much market power does the competitor have and how does he scale his business?

Growth: How has the competitor´s growth changed in the past and how is it likely to change in the future?

COMPETITOR **GAINS**

WHAT IS THE ADVANTAGE OF THIS COMPETITOR?

Products: What are the product advantadges of this competitor?

Services: What are the service advantadges of this competitor?

Solutions: What are the „complete solution" advantadges of this competitor?

COMPETITOR **PAINS**

WHAT IS THE DISADVANTAGE OF THIS COMPETITOR?

Products: What are the product advantadges of this competitor?

Services: What are the service advantadges of this competitor?

Solutions: What are the „complete solution“ advantadges of this competitor?

MOST ATTRACTIVE **ALTERNATIVES**

NOTE THE BEST PRODUCT ALTERNATIVES TO YOUR PRODUCT

A-Level: What is the BEST Product ALTERNATIVE of this competitor to your PRODUCT?

B-Level: What is an ACCEPTABLE Product ALTERNATIVE of this competitor to your PRODUCT?

C-Level: What is a TOLERABLE Product ALTERNATIVE of this competitor to your PRODUCT?

ALTERNATIVE **OPTIONS**

NOTE ADVANTAGES AND DISADVANTAGES of the ALTERNATIVES

A-Level: What are the advantages and disadvantages of the alternative products?

B-Level: What are the advantages and disadvantages of the alternative products?

C-Level: What are the advantages and disadvantages of the alternative products?

COMPETITOR CANVAS

B-LEVEL COMPETITOR

Priority PRIMARY

NAME:

FOUNDATION:

EMPLOYEES:

PRODUCTS:

MONEY:

“ VISION ”

Mission: The mission, that needs to be done?

CEO AND DRIVER

WHO IS THE DRIVER IN THIS COMPANY

Priority PRIMARY

NAME:

AGE:

OCCUPATION:

LOCATION:

INCOME:

“ Statement ”

Job to be done: The persona job, that needs to be done?

HIS MISSION: Why he is the DRIVER in this company?

COMPETITOR STRATEGY

HOW DOES THE COMPETITOR RECH ITS CUSTOMERS?

STRATEGY: What is the competitor´s market strategy?

MARKETING: Which marketing strategy does the competitor pursue?

PARTNER: Which partners does the competitor work with?

COMPETITOR MARKET AND SIZE

WHAT IS THE DISADVANTAGE OF THIS COMPETITOR?

MARKETS: Which markets does the competitor own or try to occupy? In which markets is he active?

SIZE & SCALING: How much market power does the competitor have and how does he scale his business?

Growth: How has the competitor´s growth changed in the past and how is it likely to change in the future?

COMPETITOR **GAINS**

WHAT IS THE ADVANTAGE OF THIS COMPETITOR?

Products: What are the product advantadges of this competitor?

Services: What are the service advantadges of this competitor?

Solutions: What are the „complete solution“ advantadges of this competitor?

COMPETITOR **PAINS**

WHAT IS THE DISADVANTAGE OF THIS COMPETITOR?

Products: What are the product advantadges of this competitor?

Services: What are the service advantadges of this competitor?

Solutions: What are the „complete solution“ advantadges of this competitor?

MOST ATTRACTIVE **ALTERNATIVES**

NOTE THE BEST PRODUCT ALTERNATIVES TO YOUR PRODUCT

A-Level: What is the BEST Product ALTERNATIVE of this competitor to your PRODUCT?

B-Level: What is an ACCEPTABLE Product ALTERNATIVE of this competitor to your PRODUCT?

C-Level: What is a TOLERABLE Product ALTERNATIVE of this competitor to your PRODUCT?

ALTERNATIVE **OPTIONS**

NOTE ADVANTAGES AND DISADVANTAGES of the ALTERNATIVES

A-Level: What are the advantages and disadvantages of the alternative products?

B-Level: What are the advantages and disadvantages of the alternative products?

C-Level: What are the advantages and disadvantages of the alternative products?

COMPETITOR CANVAS

B-LEVEL COMPETITOR

Priority Secondary

NAME:

FOUNDATION:

EMPLOYEES:

PRODUCTS:

MONEY:

“ VISION ”

Mission: The mission, that needs to be done?

CEO AND DRIVER

WHO IS THE DRIVER IN THIS COMPANY

Priority PRIMARY

NAME:

AGE:

OCCUPATION:

LOCATION:

INCOME:

“ Statement

”

Job to be done: The persona job, that needs to be done?

HIS MISSION: Why he is the DRIVER in this company?

COMPETITOR STRATEGY

HOW DOES THE COMPETITOR RECH ITS CUSTOMERS?

STRATEGY: What is the competitor´s market strategy?

MARKETING: Which marketing strategy does the competitor pursue?

PARTNER: Which partners does the competitor work with?

COMPETITOR **MARKET AND SIZE**

WHAT IS THE DISADVANTAGE OF THIS COMPETITOR?

MARKETS: Which markets does the competitor own or try to occupy? In which markets is he active?

SIZE & SCALING: How much market power does the competitor have and how does he scale his business?

Growth: How has the competitor´s growth changed in the past and how is it likely to change in the future?

COMPETITOR GAINS

WHAT IS THE ADVANTAGE OF THIS COMPETITOR?

Products: What are the product advantadges of this competitor?

Services: What are the service advantadges of this competitor?

Solutions: What are the „complete solution“ advantadges of this competitor?

COMPETITOR **PAINS**

WHAT IS THE DISADVANTAGE OF THIS COMPETITOR?

Products: What are the product advantadges of this competitor?

Services: What are the service advantadges of this competitor?

Solutions: What are the „complete solution“ advantadges of this competitor?

MOST ATTRACTIVE ALTERNATIVES

NOTE THE BEST PRODUCT ALTERNATIVES TO YOUR PRODUCT

A-Level: What is the BEST Product ALTERNATIVE of this competitor to your PRODUCT?

B-Level: What is an ACCEPTABLE Product ALTERNATIVE of this competitor to your PRODUCT?

C-Level: What is a TOLERABLE Product ALTERNATIVE of this competitor to your PRODUCT?

ALTERNATIVE OPTIONS

NOTE ADVANTAGES AND DISADVANTAGES of the ALTERNATIVES

A-Level: What are the advantages and disadvantages of the alternative products?

B-Level: What are the advantages and disadvantages of the alternative products?

C-Level: What are the advantages and disadvantages of the alternative products?

COMPETITOR CANVAS

C-LEVEL COMPETITOR

NAME:

FOUNDATION:

EMPLOYEES:

PRODUCTS:

MONEY:

“ VISION ”

Mission: The mission, that needs to be done?

CEO AND DRIVER

WHO IS THE DRIVER IN THIS COMPANY

Priority PRIMARY

NAME:

AGE:

OCCUPATION:

LOCATION:

INCOME:

“ Statement ”

Job to be done: The persona job, that needs to be done?

HIS MISSION: Why he is the DRIVER in this company?

COMPETITOR **STRATEGY**

HOW DOES THE COMPETITOR RECH ITS CUSTOMERS?

STRATEGY: What is the competitor´s market strategy?

MARKETING: Which marketing strategy does the competitor pursue?

PARTNER: Which partners does the competitor work with?

COMPETITOR **MARKET AND SIZE**

WHAT IS THE DISADVANTAGE OF THIS COMPETITOR?

MARKETS: Which markets does the competitor own or try to occupy? In which markets is he active?

SIZE & SCALING: How much market power does the competitor have and how does he scale his business?

Growth: How has the competitor´s growth changed in the past and how is it likely to change in the future?

COMPETITOR **GAINS**

WHAT IS THE ADVANTAGE OF THIS COMPETITOR?

Products: What are the product advantadges of this competitor?

Services: What are the service advantadges of this competitor?

Solutions: What are the „complete solution" advantadges of this competitor?

COMPETITOR PAINS

WHAT IS THE DISADVANTAGE OF THIS COMPETITOR?

Products: What are the product advantadges of this competitor?

Services: What are the service advantadges of this competitor?

Solutions: What are the „complete solution" advantadges of this competitor?

MOST ATTRACTIVE ALTERNATIVES

NOTE THE BEST PRODUCT ALTERNATIVES TO YOUR PRODUCT

A-Level: What is the BEST Product ALTERNATIVE of this competitor to your PRODUCT?

B-Level: What is an ACCEPTABLE Product ALTERNATIVE of this competitor to your PRODUCT?

C-Level: What is a TOLERABLE Product ALTERNATIVE of this competitor to your PRODUCT?

ALTERNATIVE OPTIONS

NOTE ADVANTAGES AND DISADVANTAGES of the ALTERNATIVES

A-Level: What are the advantages and disadvantages of the alternative products?

B-Level: What are the advantages and disadvantages of the alternative products?

C-Level: What are the advantages and disadvantages of the alternative products?

MARKETS

- What do the markets look like?
- How big and how much are the markets changing?
- Which branches are occupied and which are open?
- What are the alternatives?

WHAT ARE THE BIGGEST MARKETS?

IN WHICH MARKETS WILL THE PRODUCT BE IN DEMAND?

A-LEVEL market / primary

GROWTH

SIZE

A-LEVEL market / primary

GROWTH

SIZE

A-LEVEL market / secondary

GROWTH

SIZE

B-LEVEL market / primary

SIZE

B-LEVEL market / secondary

SIZE

C-LEVEL markets

MARKET CANVAS

A-LEVEL MARKET

Priority PRIMARY

NAME:

DEMAND:

COUNTRY:

LEADER:

SIZE:

“ VISION ”

Mission: The mission, that needs to be done?

POSITIONING THE PRODUCT

WHERE EXACTLY IS THE PRODUCT POSITIONED?

BRANCH: In which industries will the product be used?

Customer Groups: Which customer groups will use the product?

PARALLELS: Which parallel products exist to the product?

ALTERNATIVES: Which alternative products exist?

FINAL BRANCH: Which final branch ist the right for your product?

DEMOGRAPHIC TRENDS

LOOK for data on demographics, education, employment, etc.

DEMOGRAPHIC TRENDS: What are the most important demographic trends?

CONCLUSION: What is your conclusion?

RULES & REGULATIONS

ARE THERE TRENDS THAT WILL IMPACT YOUR BUSINESS?

RULES & REGULATIONS: What are the most important rules & regulation trends?

CONCLUSION: What is your conclusion?

ECONOMY

TRENDS IN THE ECONOMY THAT WILL IMPACT YOUR BUSINESS

ECONOMY: What are the most important ECONOMY trends?

CONCLUSION: What is your conclusion?

ENVIRONMENT

TRENDS IN ENVIRONMENT THAT WILL IMPACT YOUR BUSINESS

ENVIRONMENT: What are the most important trends in your environment?

CONCLUSION: What is your conclusion?

COMPETITION

WHAT TRENDS DO YOU SEE AMONG YOUR COMPETITORS?

COMPETITION: What are the most important trends that will influence your competitors?

CONCLUSION: What is your conclusion?

TECHNOLOGY

TRENDS IN TECHNOLOGY THAT WILL IMPACT YOUR BUSINESS

TECHNOLOGY: What are the most important technology trends that will influence your business?

CONCLUSION: What is your conclusion?

CUSTOMER NEEDS

WHAT ARE THE BIG TRENDS IN CUSTOMER NEEDS?

CUSTOMER NEEDS: What are the strongest trends affecting your customers and their needs?

CONCLUSION: What is your conclusion?

UNCERTAINTIES

DO YOU SEE ANY BIG UNCERTAINTIES?

UNCERTAINTIES: What are the biggest uncertainties you see overall in your business of on the market?

CONCLUSION: What is your conclusion?

PRODUCT

- What does the product vision look like?
- What are the benefits of the product?
- How does the product differentiate itself from alternatives?

PRODUCT BOARD

WHAT IS THE PURPOSE FOR CREATING THE PRODUCT?

Product Vision

NAME:

TYPE:

...:

“ VISION

”

Value: Explain, what is the most important benefit of the product for the customer?

THE **BIGGEST EPICS** OF THE PRODUCT?

WRITE DOWN THE BIGGEST EPICS / USECASES OF THE PRODUCT

PRODUCT BOARD

WHAT IS THE PURPOSE FOR CREATING THE PRODUCT?

NEEDS: Which customer problems does the problem solve?

PRODUCT: What makes the product stand out?

BUSINESS GOALS: How is the product going to benefit the company?

Customer View

Product View

Business View

PRODUCT INFORMATION

WHAT DO YOU NEED TO PROMOTE THE PRODUCT

WEBSITE: Which message must the website deliver?

CHANNELS: Which channels can you use?

PAPERS: Which papers do you need to provide?

REPRESENTATIVE: Which influencers can you win for the product?

VALUE PROPOSITION

HOW DOES THE PRODUCT CREATE VALUE FOR THE CUSTOMER?

CUSTOMERS JOB: What do the customer's tasks look like?

PAINS: What are the challenges for the customer?

GAINS: What solutions do customers expect from the product?

PRODUCT: What products or services do I offer to help my client complete tasks?

PAIN RELIEVERS: How do I put an end to the difficulties and challenges of my customers?

GAIN CREATORS: With what and how do I meet customer needs?

PRODUCT **CONSTRUCTION**

WHAT DO YOU NEED TO PRODUCE THE PRODUCT

RESSOURCES: Which components do you need to produce the product?

ENVIRONMENT: Which technical environment and technology do you need to produce the product?

PEOPE: Which kind and how many of people do you need to produce the product?

QUALIFICATION AND METHODS: Which qualifications and methods do you need to produce the product?

PRODUCT **SELLING**

WHAT DO YOU NEED TO SELL THE PRODUCT

RESSOURCES: Which components do you need to sell the product?

ENVIRONMENT: Which technical environment and technology do you need to sell the product?

PEOPE: Which kind and how many of people do you need to sell the product?

QUALIFICATION AND METHODS: Which qualifications and methods do you need to sell the product?

PRODUCT **FINANCE**

HOW DO YOU ASSESS THE FINANCIAL SITUATION?

SALES VOLUME: What quantity of products will you sell?

t

REVENTUE: How much will you achieve with the product?

t

COST: How high will the costs for the quantity sold be?

t

PROFIT: How much profit will the quantity sold generate?

t

PRODUCT **NOTES**

IS THERE ANYTHING IMPORTANT TO NOTE DOWN?

NOTES: Is there anything IMPORTANT to note down?

PARTNER

- What kind of partners do I need?
- What services do partners provide?
- What benefits do partners bring me?
- How can I imitate partner services?

WHAT SERVICES DO YOU NEED?

WHICH SERVICES DO YOU NEED FOR YOUR BUSINESS?

SERVICES in selling, marketing, social media and internet

SERVICES in qualification, education & people management

SERVICES in storage, hosting, delivery and transportation

SERVICES in finance, tax and law

SERVICES in ressources, technology & scaling

SERVICES in research & development

WHAT ARE THE BEST PARTNERS?

WHICH PARTNERS DO YOU NEED & WHICH CAN HELP YOU BEST?

PARTNER in selling, marketing, social media and internet

PARTNER in qualification, education & people management

PARTNER in storage, hosting, delivery and transportation

PARTNER in finance, tax and law

PARTNER in ressources, technology & scaling

PARTNER in research & development

PARTNER CANVAS

HOW CAN THE PARTNER HELP?

NAME:

TYPE:

“ MISSION ”

Products: What products does this partner supply?

Services: What services does this partner provide?

Support: How else can this partner support?

PARTNER CANVAS

HOW CAN THE PARTNER HELP?

NAME:

TYPE:

"MISSION

"

Products: What products does this partner supply?

Services: What services does this partner provide?

Support: How else can this partner support?

PARTNER CANVAS

HOW CAN THE PARTNER HELP?

NAME:

TYPE:

“ MISSION ”

Products: What products does this partner supply?

Services: What services does this partner provide?

Support: How else can this partner support?

PARTNER CANVAS

HOW CAN THE PARTNER HELP?

NAME:

TYPE:

" MISSION

"

Products: What products does this partner supply?

Services: What services does this partner provide?

Support: How else can this partner support?

PARTNER CANVAS

HOW CAN THE PARTNER HELP?

NAME:

TYPE:

“ MISSION ”

Products: What products does this partner supply?

Services: What services does this partner provide?

Support: How else can this partner support?

PARTNER CANVAS

HOW CAN THE PARTNER HELP?

NAME:

TYPE:

“ MISSION ”

Products: What products does this partner supply?

Services: What services does this partner provide?

Support: How else can this partner support?

PARTNER CANVAS

HOW CAN THE PARTNER HELP?

NAME:

TYPE:

“ MISSION ”

Products: What products does this partner supply?

Services: What services does this partner provide?

Support: How else can this partner support?

PARTNER CANVAS

HOW CAN THE PARTNER HELP?

NAME:

TYPE:

“ MISSION ”

Products: What products does this partner supply?

Services: What services does this partner provide?

Support: How else can this partner support?

MARKETING

- How can I distribute the product?
- Which channels can I use?
- What strategies can I use?
- What platforms are available?

MARKETING BOARD

HOW IS THE PRODUCT PRESENTED TO THE WORLD?

IMAGE: What kind of image should this product embody?

VALUE: What are the benefits of the IMAGE?

IMAGE

BY WHAT MEANS IS THE IMAGE CONSTRUCTED?

CONSTRUCTION: By what means is the image constructed?

COMPONENTS

WHAT IS NEEDED TO CARRY THE IMAGE INTO THE WORLD?

COMPONENTS: What is needed to carry the image into the world?

VALUE: What are the benefits of the components?

WEBSITE

WHAT MUST THE WEBSITE ALL CONTAIN?

WEBSITE: What must the website all contain?

VALUE: What are the benefits of the website?

MARKETING **ACTIVITIES**

WHAT MARKETING ACTIVITIES ARE PLANNED?

Direct Mail: Sending letters.

E-MAIL: Email campaigns.

SOCIAL MEDIA: Facebook, Twitter, YouTube, LinkedIn, Instagram, Pinterest.

OTHER: Paper, TV, Radio...

MARKETING **KPIs**

WHICH KPIS SHOULD BE FULFILLED WHEN?

Direct Mail: Sending letters.

t

E-MAIL: Email campaigns.

t

SOCIAL MEDIA: Facebook, Twitter, YouTube, LinkedIn, Instagram, Pinterest.

t

OTHER: Paper, TV, Radio...

t

BUSINESS MODEL

What does my holistic business model look like?

BUSINESS MODEL

NOTE in SUMMARY your BUSINESS MODEL

Key Partners: ...

Key Activities: ...

Key Ressources: ...

VALUE PROPOSITION

NOTE in SUMMARY the VALUE PROPOSITION

VALUE PROPOSITION: ...

Key Activities: ...

Key Ressources: ...

BUSINESS MODEL

NOTE in SUMMARY your BUSINESS MODEL

Customer Segments: For whom are we creating value?

Customer Relationships: What type of relationship does each of our Customer Segments expect us to establish and maintain with them?

Channels: Through which Channels do our Customer Segments want to be reached?

BUSINESS MODEL

NOTE in SUMMARY your BUSINESS MODEL

SALES VOLUME: What quantity of products will you sell?

REVENTUE: How much will you achieve with the product?

COST: How high will the costs for the quantity sold be?

PROFIT: How much profit will the quantity sold generate?

Printed in Poland
by Amazon Fulfillment
Poland Sp. z o.o., Wrocław

69561677R00092